VOICES FROM INSIDE
Women Writing In Prison
an anthology

Edited by Jacqueline Sheehan

Published by Voices From Inside
under the auspices of
Amherst Writers and Artists Press, 2005.
Printed by Collective Copies, Florence, Massachusetts.

Cover art by Penni Martorell
Book design by Stevie Converse

Voices From Inside
PO Box 60443
Florence, MA 01062

ACKNOWLEDGEMENTS

The publication of an anthology from Voices From Inside has been a dream for many of us and there are many people who helped bring the project to fruition. Carolyn Benson and Sara Weinberger have guided the helm of VFI from the beginning and brought continued wisdom to the anthology. Patricia Lee Lewis offered several visionary sessions to help us picture the project. Olga Candelario translated from Spanish to English with the heart of an artist. Emily Todd, English Professor, gave generous time when legions of students beckoned her. Stevie Converse was a brilliant book designer and champion of the authors. Penni Martorell produced the cover design with such good will and empathy for the project. Many thanks to Terry Blanchard for originally designing the Voices From Inside logo.

We are grateful to The Irene E. and George A. Davis Foundation, The Icarus Foundation, The National Center for Outreach, The Gardiner Howland Shaw Foundation, The Women's Fund of Western Massachusetts, and our many individual supporters.

And most importantly, sincere thanks to the women who trusted the writing process during and after their incarceration and who have generously shared their words with us.

VOICES FROM INSIDE
Women Writing in Prison
an anthology

FROM THE EDITOR

When I first met Carolyn Benson, I underestimated her. We were attending a Patchwork Farm writing retreat on the edge of the jungle in Yelapa, Mexico. She sat in the shade with a cloth draped over her head to protect herself from the sun. Fragile, I thought. I was so wrong, so utterly wrong.

Carolyn Benson is the co-founder, with Sara Weinberger, of Voices From Inside and has run over 20 writing groups in prison. I was fortunate enough to assist her with writing groups for a year and a half. Each weekly group is ten weeks long, two hours each week. Incarcerated women came to us who may have experienced creative writing before, but more often they had not experienced writing at all and certainly not as a way to dig deep, create, and offer a piece of emotion, reflecting back to the world through the unique filter of their experience.

At first the commonality for the women seemed to be imprisonment, either serving time while awaiting trial, or serving time after sentencing. The commonality changed after the first day of writing. We were writers. For two hours each week, we were all women writing together, in Spanish and in English, writing from prompts that Carolyn and I brought to prison: a poem from Pat Schneider or Jimmy Santiago Baca, photos from magazines, simple objects from a sewing basket, or a phrase like, "what matters now." Writing in prison with these women forever dispelled the belief that writers must have a soothing environment to feed their creativity; the frequent clang of thick metal doors, locking and unlocking, the wail of a woman brought in to prison for the first time, and the ever watchful eyes scanning us on the camera provided the constant hum of our background. Not exactly the room of one's own of which Virginia Woolf wrote. But I finally understood what Carolyn was doing back in Mexico; she was not protecting her pale skin, she was planning a revolution of spirit, and the revolution was happening each week in the writing groups.

Each week the women left and returned to their cells while we gathered up their writing and carried it with us, back out through the prison checkpoints. We edited lightly, never changing a rich and unique voice that rang clear with street language, and never without the permission of the writer. We returned the following week with typed manuscripts, the original format with our comments, and an edited version with our suggestions in place. At the end of ten weeks, women selected 2-4 pieces that they wanted to submit to the chapbook that was produced by us and presented with as much pageantry as possible at their graduation ceremony.

And so it went with the other groups that other facilitators ran, some at the prison's pre-release program, another at Howard Street (a correctional alcohol center), and another in the community for newly released women. The work presented in this anthology was selected from the accumulated chapbooks from each group. Their voices in poetry and prose are not hammered fine by multiple edits, but purposely left fresh from their unique writing experience.

The reader will notice that we use only the first names of the writers from our workshops. This decision was the result of much debate. The final decision was based on the welfare of the women, who sometimes face harsh repercussions in society for serving time in prison. While most of the women would willingly and proudly use their last names, some of the women were fearful of any notoriety connected with the penal system; they worried about custody issues, immigration, and employment prospects.

The anthology begins with the history of the project from the co-founders. What follows is the powerful chorus of women writing from prison. We end the anthology with selected pieces by some of our facilitators. All proceeds from the sale of the Anthology will continue to fund more writing workshops for Voices From Inside.

Jacqueline Sheehan, October 2005

HOW WE BEGAN:
THE CO-FOUNDERS OF VOICES FROM INSIDE SPEAK

Voices From Inside is a creative writing program begun in 1999 for women who are incarcerated or have been incarcerated. Our mission is two-fold: to facilitate creative writing workshops where women prisoners and ex-prisoners can tell their own stories in their own diverse voices, and to increase public awareness of the human costs of incarceration. Located in Western Massachusetts, we currently run four groups for women: in a medium-security prison, its pre-release program, its substance abuse treatment facility, as well as a group for women recently released into the community. Each group is led by two facilitators who have been trained in the Amherst Writers & Artists method of facilitating writing groups with people from under-served populations.

> ***May 10*** *The day finally arrives! Our space, a multi-purpose room, is open and full of light. We have a bathroom, but no one is permitted to use it. Windows punctuate the inner wall so we can be seen at all times, and floor to ceiling windows look out on the courtyard where guards stand their posts and lines of men straggle*

*from one building to another. The women are not
supposed to look out the windows at the men. It's very
clear that we are with a small pocket of women in a huge
men's institution.*

The United States currently incarcerates more men
and women than any other country in the world, and the rate
of incarceration for women has increased much faster than
that of men. This is largely because of mandatory sentencing
laws that have been an outcome of the war on drugs. The
majority of women are incarcerated for non-violent, drug-
related crimes. They suffer from a whole host of problems,
including drug addiction, poverty, lack of education,
inadequate housing, childhood abuse, domestic violence,
mental illness, lack of access to adequate health care, AIDS
and HIV. Seventy-five per cent are mothers. The prison
system, which was fundamentally designed to meet the
needs of male prisoners, is not able to adequately address the
issues of the large numbers of women flooding state and
federal prisons.

*We ask each of the women to say her name
and one thing she hopes to get out of the workshop.
Most have children, many have grandchildren.
Several like to write poetry . S. says she likes to
write letters, and her friends in the pod like to hear
them before she sends them off. To my surprise the
exercise works. All but two of the women read, and
it's like watching flowers open to see their stony
faces dissolve and hear the stories pouring out.*

*<u>May 17</u> I emphasize the importance of giving
feedback to each other when we read, that this helps
all of us to see what is working. What works, what
stays with them? Then we go straight into an
exercise -- "Once I was . . . now I am . . . ." The
feedback is better this week – the women are*

beginning to mention details. They give a lot of weight to any hint of hope at the end of a piece. It will take real courage for them to write something without a happy ending.

Paper clips are contraband!

May 24 The group is smaller today. Three women don't feel well, C. and L. are locked up. It's a holiday weekend, and things are difficult around here. C.H. writes a wonderful poem about growing and selling vegetables, and as I watch her read I also see B.'s beaming face, reading along with her over her shoulder. It is like a miracle to see that much pleasure over something just created in our workshop. What they write soars and sings so eloquently – I want the world to hear these voices!

Disruptive behaviors, apathy, poor attendance, tardiness, recidivism, conflicts among group members, writing deficits, are all factors that challenge people who lead the writing groups for incarcerated women. Providing group facilitators with information about the criminal justice system and the effect that it can have on women, is essential. Our facilitators are required to attend in-service training programs and supervision meetings that provide information as well as support.

May 31 H. is having trouble with the side-effects of her medication. The writing is deeper, and very good. J.A. reads a wonderful piece about listening to music with her children. I realize that the joy of writing for the women in the workshop is not only the pleasure of remembering, but also the pleasure of sharing their memories.

The rapid growth of the prison-industrial complex in the United States has been supported by a culture that views punishment as the necessary response to criminal behavior. People who commit crimes are viewed as the "other" and are set apart from the rest of society, both physically and psychologically. When society does not put a human face on the people who are incarcerated, it can continue to ignore the rights of a whole group of people to be treated with dignity. Prison uniforms, line-ups, bed-checks and searches, even when necessary, serve to reinforce for women in prison the message that they are bad people who do not deserve to be treated with dignity.

> <u>June 7</u>   *Sometimes the institution itself overshadows our work. We can see the infantilizing effects on the women of having every aspect of their lives controlled by others.*
>
> *They are free to go back to their residential units to use the toilet, but there's no guarantee they will be allowed back out to our workshop. The women pretty much know what they can do, depending on which Correctional Officer (CO) is on duty. If I have to use the bathroom during the two-hour class I have to find a CO to unlock the door.*
>
> *For the exercise, I read "In Ten Years," a poem by Melissa Plumadore. The women are very moved by it, and their writing is excellent. J. writes the most wonderful piece to Melissa. "Lets sit together," she begins, and goes on to describe the cycles of a woman's life in which abuse dominates. It's as if she is speaking to her younger self. J. is dealing with issues around domestic violence. Her neck is in a brace—an old injury, she said. She is my current hero.*

Facilitators belong to a society that views women in prison as dangerous, hostile people who need to be locked away. Our first facilitators were from academic, human services or creative arts backgrounds. Then, as our groups reached more and more women, we were able to fund Amherst Writers & Artists training for formerly incarcerated women, more and more of whom are taking over as facilitators. Group facilitators participate in the writing exercises and read their writing along with group members. Writing together yields common themes such as love and concern for family members, painful relationships, regret, and a desire for growth and love. The distinction between who is inside and who is outside blurs away as people connect with one another through their writing.

> _June 14_ _For the first exercise I ask them to imagine going back in time and into a hallway between two rooms. This produces some good writing, but several have difficulty with "flashbacks." I know that over 80% of the women in this prison are self-reported victims of physical and/or sexual abuse. I wonder which exercises are most likely to bring up difficult memories? I am relieved that several were able to say they didn't want to participate in the exercise._
>
> _We spend some time talking about which of their poetry and prose will go into the graduation booklet. And I tell them I am making them certificates — they were thrilled that they are going to be certified as "genuine writers."_

When prison officials were made aware of the graduation booklets, they adopted a policy that required a prison administrator to review all pieces of writing that were to go into each booklet. References to drug use, as well as language that was considered offensive or sexually explicit have often been censored from the final compilation. This directly conflicts with VFI's emphasis on empowering members to write in their own voices. Voices From Inside staff have taken on the role of being strong advocates for retaining members' words when such situations have occurred.

June 28 *We can see anxiety building in the women who are about to go home -- B. looks tense and white; J. is testy; and J.A. tells of her fears about going home later this summer with an abusive ex-husband around, a man who has even attacked her in the visitors' room and had to be pulled off by a C.O.*

July 1 *The facility is holding a graduation for women who have completed three other programs and our writing workshop. As soon as we get there we learn that J. is in the hole (solitary confinement). We are heartsick. What does being in prison do to a woman who has a history of being abused by men? Then we found out that J.A. is also in the hole—she's always being put in for something. M. read J.A.'s poem "Caged Eagle" with its author in solitary.*

Many women in prison suffer from major mental health issues, but when women exhibit problematic behaviors, the response is usually a punitive one. As a result it's not surprising for a group facilitator to come to a meeting and discover that an active group member has been sent to solitary confinement and is thus forbidden to attend the writing workshop. There is a gap between the prison culture that is based on rules and conformity, and the culture of creative writing groups that is based on creativity and trust.

July 14 *J. is still in the hole and her parole has been taken away. B. and S. have gone home, D. is in pre-release. The women who are left have prepared a big thank you card for us, plus our own certificate for being good workshop leaders! C.H. wrote a long story about what it was like to grow up as the child of an alcoholic father—it's truly wonderful, a break-*

through for her. She tells us that she never knew she could write, and now she's deeply committed to being a writer. L. wrote an astonishing piece about an elderly African-American woman with dry, cracked hands, where she, who is Caucasian, completely entered the woman's life. Really good work. I'm seeing how effectively the workshop has encouraged the women to write. Even when they take exercises back to their cells and work in isolation, they are anticipating the warm welcome their work will receive from the group.

With tears and hugs we say goodbye.

Although our facilitators don't pretend or want to be therapists, they see great evidence of healing. A VFI graduate who has been out of prison for two years credits her participation in the creative writing program for her successful adjustment to life on the outside. She says it enabled her to give voice to painful feelings she'd held back since early childhood. The writing group was the only place where she felt truly free, where her writing would take her anywhere she wanted to be. She continues to write in her journal twice a day.

Voices From Inside works to build bridges of understanding between those on the inside and those on the outside by arranging for women to read their writing in colleges and universities and other public settings. When women who have been incarcerated read about their children, their own childhoods, their hopes and dreams, their searches for love and connection, the listener begins to see them as individuals. Students, many of whom are preparing for careers in human services or criminal justice, begin to recognize that we all make bad decisions, but for some the consequences can be much more devastating. The women are defined by their humanity rather than simply by behaviors that society defines as criminal.

Building bridges of connection and understanding is critical in order to remove legal, social, and economic barriers that prevent prisoners from successfully re-entering the families and communities from which they have been separated. Public readings that stimulate open discussion can motivate people to consider community based alternatives to incarceration that provide treatment for their addiction, opportunities for healthy parenting, physical and mental health treatment, job training, and education, all without the stigma of incarceration.

The goal of our public readings and the publication of this, our first anthology, is not only to change the community outside the prison walls, but to continue the process of transformation for the women writers. By making their words available to more and more people we are saying, "Your stories count, you voices will be heard."

Carolyn Benson and Sara Weinberger
Co-founders and directors of Voices From Inside
October 2005

Jail: The Graveyard of the Living Dead

As I sit in my cell I think of the forces of darkness that afflict
me with pain. What happened to society, my loved ones?
I'm forgotten. I'm not dead. People gave up on us.

Here I sit betrayed and forgotten.
I sit here lonely. I'm not rotten.
I've let go of the bondage that held me hostage.
I look to the Lord, he restored my sanity.
No more pain. No more sorrow.
Yesterday is gone, on with tomorrow.
I'm here in the graveyard of the living dead.
Visit me, write me, don't beat me in the head.
I know I'll never hear from you until I'm dead.
Forgive me. I'm sorry, I'm ashamed.
Don't you remember my name?
Now that I'm here nothing is the same.
I sit here in hope. I'm off the dope.
I need you for real. So what's the deal?
Can I hear from you soon? I feel so doomed.
I'll keep the faith and wait each day,
for you to remember I'm still away.
Among the living dead is where I lay.
Write me, visit me, please.
I'm down on my knees.
I love you, I miss you, believe me this time please.
I'm alive, I'm not dead.
I'm hard-headed and misled.
I'm alive, I'm not dead.

Paula

Scared

I was really scared when I came to jail,
not scared of the time I was facing,
not scared of the guards,
or the cell doors slamming shut,
not even scared of the stories
I was told about jail.
I was really scared when I was told
that I wouldn't see my children
for five long years.
I was really scared when I was put
in a bright orange uniform
and told to call my family and pray
like hell that they'd accept a collect call.

I was really scared when I couldn't sleep
in a small cell with two other females,
not knowing if I'd wake up to another day.
I was really scared when I remembered
I had forgotten to pray.
I guess when I really take a look back,
I was really scared
when I committed the crime.
Come to think of it,
I was really scared of doing time.

Tina

The Quietest Time

The quietest time was when everyone was asleep,
for that's the best time of day, when everyone
can do the same thing and all get along.
You don't hear no complaining, gossip or foul mouth.
All you hear is snoring or grinding of teeth.
All through the night you hear keys in the door
waking you from your sleep only to realize
it's the R.S. checking to see if you're alright,
but it seems to disturb me every single night.
I have a problem with someone opening the door
especially when I look up and there is a man
standing there just doing his job.
I feel it's quite annoying.

Linda

Is This What I Want?

Is this what I want? To be told what time I can walk out of
my room door? To be told what days I can shave and I can't
shower after 11 pm? What I can eat and when I can eat it?
Not to be able to hold my loved ones when I want to and
only see them for an hour? Is this what I want, not to be able
to wear what I want? Is this what I really want, to be around
women or anyone in general that if you say anything about
your case they can use it against you for a smaller bid? To be
told when I can go home, if possible, and what I can and
cannot do when I get there? Is this what I want?

Joana

We Would Like You to Know

We would like you to know that we are inmates
but also decent women.
We would like you to know that just because
we were behind walls
that don't mean you can't respect us for who we are.
We would like you to know that we are also human beings
and deserve a chance because nobody's perfect.
We would like you to know that we are not proud
and we are looking for help.
We would like you to know that we are smart
and have a lot to offer.
We would like you to know that we all did a crime
and we are doing our time.
We would like you to know that with the help
of the Almighty God we will see the sunlight
and reunite with our loved ones
because we didn't kill anybody,
so they can't keep us here for life.
We would like you to know that shit happens in life,
but we are very strong women
and we will get through these rough times.
We would like you to know so you will stop
treating us like trash because although we are inmates,
we are women with pride.

Jessica

On Either Side

All I need to do is to have the strength
to take one more step.
One more step
and I'll be on my own.

But I'm scared!!
What awaits me out there?

One more step
and I'll be out these doors...
Out these doors of loneliness...
Out these doors of hearing other people crying out in pain
because they miss their loved ones,
or because their bodies need a fix.

Out these doors...
where one is told when to eat, sleep, and even shower...
Out these doors...
where one's superiors belittle us.
Out these doors...
that have keys to keep us in.
I'm done.
I'm done living inside of these doors.

What's out there on the other side of these doors?
Poverty and hunger...
Drugs and sex...
Lovers who beat you...
Family that betrays you...
Children who are rude and have no respect...
Adults that just don't care if they cause others pain...
Politics that are corrupted along with all other systems.
Where do I go?

Where do I run to?
I don't want to go out these doors.
Nor do I want to stay in these doors.

Allison

C10, cell 41

My cell was dirty, so I cleaned it.
My cell was lonely, so I asked for a roommate.
My cell was depressing, so I cried.
My cell was dark, so I stayed on the top bunk under the light.
My cell was boring, so I read lots of books.
My cell was too quiet, so I sang.
My cell made me think, so I started writing.
My cell faced an empty field, so I watched the rabbits.
My cell took my mobility but not my mind.
My cell was just a small room with a locked door.
My cell was no longer mine when the C.O. said, "pack it up."
My cell was someplace I never want to be again.

Frances

A World Without Prisons

I can't even imagine a world without prisons. Where would all the bad people like me go? After all, I'm addicted to illegal drugs. That makes me bad. I've done other illegal activities to obtain these drugs. That makes me bad. After all this is the place I'll get help, perhaps even get well is it not?! My children will be taken away, that will surely help. My family will disown me. That will no doubt make me feel loved, therefore I'll use all the things available to get better so I can rush home, home to a place no longer open to me. Hey, not to mention all the opportunities open to me once I'm finally released. So yeah, I can't imagine a world without prisons. After all where would all us bad people go?!

Patricia

ADDICTION

Once I Was Naked

Once I was naked from beauty.
Once I was touched by his hand,
that wiped a tear from my lonely eyes.

Once I was robbed from laughter of sad darkened flesh.
Once I was the door that got slammed over and over.
Once I was the heroin addict
With the scars on my veins.

Now I'm dressed with this everlasting life.
Now I touch with my own palms and
Wipe my own tears with my hands.
Now I steal my own laughter.
Now I'm the one slamming the door.
Now I'm the one who can taste day in the air
without heroin.

Toni

Letter

Dear Debra,

You don't know who I am but I want you to know I am a friend. I want to tell you that it's not cool to smoke and the beer you drink behind your Dad's back could end up getting worse and that's a fact. I'm an alcoholic/addict if you don't know what that is it's a person who can't stop drinking alcohol or use drugs. I want to help you at your age and I want to tell you to be careful who you play with. They will get you to do drugs and steal from stores and get drunk under the bridge. They might want you to have sex so tell them no! Debra, you're just ten years old. My parents never told me about sex, drugs, or alcohol. That's why I write to you to let you know.

I'm thirty years old and I sit in jail for shooting heroin and stealing from people, stores and homes. I've gotten my freedom taken away from me. I know you're a smart girl and I know you understand. You watch T.V. and that's where you see a lot of bad things that happen to people.

Yes, I'm one of those bad people, but I'm getting better. I want to tell you, Debra, please use your mind and do what is right because if you're confused or in a bad situation just say no and go home or tell someone who can help you. Don't be afraid or run away. This letter is to let you know that I want to be there for you when you're afraid. I know your parents don't speak to you about things and that's why I wanted to write to let you know that I will understand and I don't want you to run away.

Your friend,
Honesty

Debra

Did They Forget About Me?

Did they forget about me? No, I'm sure they haven't, I know they're thinking, *"Pennie gets out of jail this month so I'll call up her mom and leave a number so she'll think she's been in my best thoughts. I know after all this time Pennie wants a nice drink of gin and a big hit of crack. And while she's smoking it, I know my trick is done. Now she'll be stuck in this valley of drugs with me, because I love her and I never stopped thinking about her. While I was using, she was getting rest and new refreshed brain cells to destroy."*

But no way, I have a next plan. Although I called my so called lover, I knew her plan, so I spoke to her as she spoke to me, telling me how things were and that I actually should stay away from her because she's no good for me. Well I do know that she's not, but somehow I think I still love her too, but no, I can't lie; I still love the drugs, I'll always love them, it comes with my addiction to drugs. My disease has never forgotten about me. Now I choose my life.

Pennie

Freedom

Freedom is the grass under
Your toes,
The coolest of waters you can feel
Flowing through your soul,
Y'know.

It's a hawk soaring
In the sky
Or when a baby cries for the
Very first time.

Freedom for me, I almost forgot
When I picked up that
Needle and shot.
I believed that feeling was
Something so free,
But in the end it almost
Killed me.

Now I sit behind this
Wall
With no freedom at all.

Kathy Jo

Things I've Learned

I've learned that a wire hanger is called a "pimp stick."
The thin metal is straightened out, heated on the stove, and
applied to the bare thigh. Branded.

I've learned that the best time to hustle on the street is during
the shift change of local law enforcement. They stagger the
turnover in intervals and you have to be aware, but
it's the best time to trick or score dope.

I've learned that my college education is not totally
useless on the whore stroll. Some tricks are amazed
and even impressed, and will come back to be entertained by
the hooker with the heroin habit who can quote Eliot,
Whitman, and Thoreau.

I've learned that I become invisible to people I used to know,
to my own family, and to God Himself. To acknowledge me
would be to acknowledge my failings and my suffering.
Such things are best left unnoticed.

I've learned that addiction, poverty, and ignorance are
not contagious, but fear is.
I've learned that the difference between walking and running
is who's behind you.
I thought I knew everything. I've learned that I know
nothing.

Dede

Right Here In Our Own Backyard Are...

Junkies, whores, and crackheads.
—Legislators, lawyers, and nurses.
Thieves, rapists, and hit men.
—Accountants, clergy, and college students.
Deviants, drunks, and child abusers.
—Policemen, doctors, and executives.
Porn peddlers, speed freaks, and perverts.
—Big business, social workers, and bank tellers.

In everybody's backyard there are—
Legislators who are crackheads.
Junkies who are lawyers, clergy who are rapists,
and doctors who peddle porn. Social workers as
speed freaks, bank tellers as child abusers,
and big businesses that thieve.
I think maybe...
It's time to clean up the backyard.

Dede

My Personal Ad: The One You Want to Bring Home to Mother

I'm an unemployable female,
chronic alcoholic, drug addict.
No children (they've been taken away).
In jail now, but I'm available
this summer. Better hurry!
I may be snatched up right away.
That is if I make parole.

Anonymous

What I Want My Words to Do to You

I want my words to tell the story of a girl who began life
with dreams like fairy tales but whose life was interrupted
by something bigger and stronger. I want you to know
how someone could feel so angry she could easily kill
or feel so sad she could never stop weeping.

How does a girl raised in the suburbs by two hard-working
parents end up shooting heroin into her arm
in the basement of a tenement in the flats?
If you looked at this family, you'd ask yourself,
how does one of three kids end up in and out
of drug addiction and jail, while the other two
become so successful and worthy of praise?

If you looked at them and did not ask that question,
it's because you don't really want to know the answer.

I want my words to wake you up.
I want my words to keep me awake.

Moana

To My Addiction
Hi and Goodbye

When we first met I fell in love
with you. I told myself we were
going to be good friends. As time
went by I became your slave,
you became my master.
I wish we never met.
You took my Self, my pride
and self-esteem. You took my
loved ones too. I did not know better.
To love you and believe in
you when I knew you were nothing
but a lie. But I was still willing to
be with you. You did nothing but
get me abused and raped. I was
yours for 25 years.
I married you because
I did not know better. Every time I
tried to run from you and get help, you
always got in my way and lied to me
again by keeping us a secret.
It's sad that it took all these years to know you.
So it's time to say goodbye for
good, my destruction, my love—I hate you.
I'm grateful today because I know
your game. Thank God for
helping me
to wake up and get you out of my life.

Rosa

One Warm Summer Evening

My first drunk was also my first time in a bar. The name of the bar was the Tavern at the Bridge and it overlooked the Merrimac River. I remember that day very well. I was walking down the street eating the pears I had just bought from the store. It was about 5:00 pm and there was a warm summer wind blowing. I was wearing black shorts and a white tank top. As I was walking I heard music coming from the bar across the street. The song was *Love Can Move Mountains*. I had been clean and sober for a while and had not thought about having a drink that day until that moment. Little did I know that this warm summer evening in July would be the beginning of a disastrous relapse. The relapse went on for about 6 weeks and my guardian angel must have been watching over me because I could have died in any one of the many dangerous situations I put myself in. I'm very blessed that I got yet another chance.

Michelle

Untitled

It was a nice December day
Clear, cool and snowing lightly.
The sun was shining brightly.
I should look out the window and be
at peace, but I look inside
and find turmoil.
I found a bottle from last night
Shall I think it through and do what's right?
Maybe a little will make me forget.
I have some and think I'm all set.
No, I must get some more
I said to myself as I reached the door.
In the car and to the store.
I have a bad feeling down to my core.
Got in the car and started home.
Snow is still coming down lightly
Better put on the brakes slightly

Can't control the skid anymore
Hit another car's door.
My head is so sore.

Ambulance, police, people upside down
Am I flying in the sky?

Anonymous

The Show

I feel lost when I walk the streets. It's no different from childhood. Who cares about the age? Not them, I've lived it since age 12.

Lost, lonely, scared, fearing the man that will hold me and lay his body on mine, night after night. Not choosing one till I was so inebriated they look good.
Me, young, homeless, abused day after day since age three, drinking and drugging 'til I didn't know any better. Sex with another unknown, just to be able to eat, sleep and live.

Gone to jail once, twice, three times…or was it four or five? The last ride, you whore, you crack-head drunk, living life in the fast lane, like you have a license or something.

Living life like a card game at the casino, a game of Russian Roulette, or living the day of Halloween, a trick the disease.

Oh, here we go again, feeling like I'm on *Jeopardy*, how about *The Price is Right*, or *Fear Factor*. Or maybe I'm in a puppet show, or simply the magic man's trick.

All the dollars I've received for these games and shows have gone up in smoke.

Lisa

Scars of Truth

I burn deep in my soul with secrets untold.
I let you beat me,
then I allowed you to lay your bare skin on me
while you raped me as I lay there a rag doll.
I've allowed you to burn me with cigarettes.
I'm ashamed of my body now
because of scars you have left me to tell.
I can't even let who I'm with now see my body.

He says I'm beautiful.
Yeah, just wait till I'm naked and the lights are on.
Run for you life because it's not a pretty sight.

I burn deep in my soul with secrets untold.
All my hate and misunderstandings are bottled up.
Nowhere to run, nowhere to hide, too embarrassed to cry,
I don't want anyone to ask why.

Locked behind a bathroom door,
after a drunken stupor,
I feel I just want to die,
but that would be too easy or simple.
I'd be a coward taking the easy way out.
So the next best thing that makes me feel good
and only reasonable in my eyes,
that's worked before,
is to bleed my pain off. Yeah, (sigh)

The razor injects deeply and slowly into my skin.
Gliding down my arms, the blood begins
to seep to the surface.
Dripping gently, drop by drop, it relieves
the pain of my life's crazy encounters.

I love you.
I love the razor,
but I love myself more,
so I threw you **both** out the door.
Peace.

Lisa

The Alphabet of Recovery

A -   Awareness; Attention to detail.
B -   Bold; Be yourself.
C -   Courageous; Centered; Chance.
D -   Determined; Dignified; Dream; Discovery.
E -   Eliminate negativity; Equality; Explore.
F -   Fun with friends.
G -   Good habits; Great attitude; Give back.
H -   Have fun; Don't be too serious; Humbleness.
I -   Interact; I am worth it.
J -   Joy; Just don't quit; Just for today.
K -   Kindness.
L -   Love; Laughter; Learn.
M -   Make new friends; Motivate.
N -   Never forget where you came from.
O -   Open-mindedness; One day at a time.
P -   Patience; Persevere.
Q -   Quiet the mind.
R -   Reason with yourself and others; Recovery.
S -   Spirituality; Search for peace; Seek to find who you are.
T -   Tranquility; Take care of yourself; Trust others.
U -   Understanding.
V -   Vigilance; Visible to all.
W -   Willingness; Wake your heart.
X -   Go the extra mile.
Y -   Youthful at heart.
Z -   Zest for life.

Cynthia

I won't go back there this time...
--After Pat Schneider

I won't go back there
to that lonely place of despair
where floors creak, and toilets crack
where there's wax on the dressers
where mirrors are missing or broken in half
where there's choreboy and tinfoil,
where nip bottles have holes melted in them
and a stem sticking out
where the house is boarded up
and the windows are sealed shut
and everyone gathered in the cellar to hide
To that trick in the car who scratched my face
and beat me for money.
To that cell to do time.
I won't go back to that misery of chasing that first high.
To that crazy life of chaos and unmanageability.
To that life of no self respect, no integrity, no morality,
and no personality.
I'd only end up fiending, broke, and in trouble.
I won't **won't** go back there this time.

Mary Ann

Talkin' to the Mirror

Here I am in this trashy bathroom,
boyfriend's room down the hall.
I drank sixteen ounces of wine, straight down
about seven hours ago, and I've just come to,
just now. Sixteen years of life on this planet
and I'm lookin' in the mirror. I don't recognize
the face looking back at me and it frightens me
because I know it must be me.
I say, "Who the heck are you?"
Forty-seven years on the planet.
I'm lookin' in the mirror,
Its reflection is fuzzy at best,
'cuz you can't have real mirrors in jail.
I recognize that face looking back at me now.
She is wherever I go, always there.
She is witness to all my secrets and dreams,
all the events of my life.
When I look deeply in her eyes
I can see that she knows the truth, has the answer.
She is at peace—not conflicted—not addicted.
She loves me unconditionally.
She has always been with me,
watched over me, prayed with me.
I recognize her now because she and I
are becoming one.

Moana

Over Time:
My Crime My Choice

My crime was being a scared child.
    By being a scared child
        I became quiet.

My crime was being so helpless.
    By being so helpless
        I became withdrawn.

My crime was having no feeling.
    By having no feeling
        I became hard.

My crime was being angry.
    By being angry
        I drank.

My crime was drunk driving.
    By drunk driving
        I went to jail.

My choice was to open up.
    By opening up
        I have freedom within.

Janet

Pin Cushions

When I first started high school back in 1979 my major
was Fashion Design. We made patterns and put them
together. We also bought patterns, cut them out and put
them together. We had a marrow machine. I thought this
was the next best thing to ice cream. What it did was smooth
the edges of the material so that it would not be all frilly.
Plus it made your sewing of the seams much easier and more
professional. I tell you, I loved this class. You could make
beautiful things if you applied yourself, and applied myself I
did.

Well, in the first year, my sophomore year, we had to
make whatever it was the instructor told you but in my
junior year you could make whatever your heart desired.
We were having a best dress competition. Whoever wore the
nicest thing in the school colors would win the prize. I
aimed to win the prize. I did!

Honey child let me tell you of the dress I made. Yes, me,
Ms. Ivey. First our school colors were blue and gold. So, I
made this halter dress made of deep blue satin. It had a
fitted waist and a full skirt. You know, the kind we, as little
girls, used to love to spin around and around then to make it
fly. We just *knew* we were pretty as princesses. Now for the
gold, I had a gold Cumberland belt and a short gold jacket
that hugged around the breast, the kind they have just
started to bring back. Anyway, I put that bad boy on and I
strutted across the stage and won. I was *so* proud of myself!

In my senior year I made a brown and black skirt suit for
our senior luncheon. It was a straight, long skirt and the
jacket was reversible. I've done several other things like
make pants, and clergymen shirts for my dad. I also made
him preaching robes. I was a great sewer. I say *was* because
I haven't made anything in over 15 years because of my
addiction.

Now that I'm clean and sober I am going to get out of here right before summer and I am going to make me some hot outfits, plus for my kids. I am going to make me and my ten year-old matching outfits and my 12 and 8 year-old sons matching outfits. I am a darned good sewer and there is no reason I can't return back to doing something positive in my life. To hell with drugs!

Ivey

One Night Can Change Your Life
or, Why Can't Some People Seem to Beat Addiction

One night can change your life forever. The reasons are unknown to you but you can meet the man of your dreams. Fall deeply in love with him. You make sweet love to one another and fall asleep. You wake up the next day to find the one you truly do love wants more than just a relationship. He also wants his drugs. So to make the man I love happy, I give him anything and everything. He gets his drugs. We stay awake to hustle to make that money so he can get that hit that makes him feel good for a whole 60 seconds. Then he chases after the hit. He'll do anything to the one he loves to get it. Even leave them for dead in an alleyway from some drug dealer he stole from. Then I come to jail for the drugs, gun and clip he left under the front seat without telling me. He left me for dead in prison, too. But that one day he walks through the gates looking all melted and skinny. I believe him 'cuz he's my drug of choice. Just to watch him leave me again to follow that crack, which is his drug of choice. And still, 'til this day, I love him as much as he loves your crack…The one night I met him my whole life has changed. And will never be the same again. We now have a daughter who just turned 14 years old who needs us. She suffers the most 'cuz of that one night with him. I'm in prison and he's still an addict to the drug crack he can't put down. Where do we stand while he's still free? We pay the price...Why can't we both beat our addiction?

Tracy

Home

This picture feels like home. I can smell Tide. I can smell Snuggle Fabric Softener. It's like a sweet breeze—bitter sweet—that I can almost taste. I can hear the sound of soft pattering along the floor, the small whispers calling my only true real name: Mommy.

I'm almost home. If I can just stay strong and push myself a little further, we'll be together again, at home. And I'll wrap them up with these towels, with the love and time that I missed.

My real name will I once more deserve and my real smile the world can once more see. I will finally be happy and home with my only true creations.

Lisa Q.

Single Parent

Right now I'm a single part-time mom.
I am a mother who sees her son three times a week.
I'm a mother who didn't think love was enough to make me happy.
I'm a mother who was born in the uptown, but chose to grow up in the slums.
I'm a mother who never once thought about anyone else's feelings until now.
I'm a mother whose high life was never worth the agony of coming down.
I'm a mother who has no idea of how to raise a boy into a good man.
I'm a mother who financially depends on my family.
I'm a mother whose only skill to make money is to take off my clothes.
I'm a mother who doesn't always speak proper English.

I'm a mother whose tears only appear after the fact.
I'm a mother who didn't experience any of her son's firsts.
I'm a mother with dreams and goals that have been largely tossed away.
I'm a mother who only wants to be the best mother that I possibly can be.
I'm a mother...or am I?

Joanna

Light of My Life

Light of my life, let me not be
 so burning a concern to you
as I seemed to have been a few
days ago, If in my whole youth
 I in my life have I ever done
anything which I admit to have
 been more sorry for than last
 night, when I left you alone.
 Now, just wanting to hide
because I'm guilty and shameful.
I just should have been there to
 give you passion and love.
 Light of my life you're
 still my son. I love you.

Lisa

Cutest Little Things

The last time I saw a tiny hair clip it was on my one year old daughter. Seeing those beautiful things in her hair suddenly made me realize how much I love to do hair and most of all how good it will make me feel if I can even put two braids in her hair. I hope I get the chance to do all of my daughters' hair, but there is a time and a place for everything. I first have to get myself together then I hope I'll be able to get my kids back and hook their hair up in all kinds of styles.

Lanette

Recuerdos de mi princesa

Esta foto me acuerda a mi niña linda cuando era más bebé.
Tan hermosa, tan risueña cuando todo para mi era incierto.
Mi niña, como ha crecido. Ya no reconozco en ella
aquellos rasgos que definían su pequeña estructura.
Ya no puedo ver en ella aquella necesidad
de sentirse amada por ese ser que la trajo al mundo.
A veces la siente tan lejos. Aunque quizás este cerca.
La distancia, como dijo alguien, es causa del olvido.
Porque ella se olvidó de ser hija
y yo quizás he olvidado el ser madre
Dentro de mí hay algo que me dice, "no, ella te espera."
Solo es que tiene que esperar
que la luna se convierta en sol
y el sol en luna.

Memories of My Princess

This photo reminds me of my pretty girl when she was more of a baby.

44

So beautiful, such smiling when everything for me was uncertain.

My girl, how she has grown. No longer do I recognize in her those characteristics that defined her small structure.

No longer can I see in her that necessity to feel loved by that being who brought her into the world.

Sometimes I feel her so far away. Although perhaps she is close. Distance, as somebody said, causes forgetfulness.

Because she forgot how to be a daughter

and I have perhaps forgotten being a mother.

Within me is something that says to me, "no, she waits for you."

The only thing is that she must wait until the sun becomes moon and the moon becomes a sun.

Yudelka
translated by Olga Candelario

El dolor de una madre

¿Quién conoce lo que hay dentro del corazón?
Nadie en el mundo puede ver lo que tu llevas por dentro.
Angustia, desesperación, anhelo, desprecio, engaño.
La gente solo ve en ti aquello que solo puede reflejar tu exterior
Pero no puede reflejar lo que lleva adentro tu alma.
Ese dolor que te quema, que te agobia y te quebranta el alma.
Ese dolor que supura como si fuera una llaga.
Si, ese dolor ardiente que te quema como una llama
es el dolor de una madre que sufre
porque de lo más dentro de su corazón
hay una voz que te dice "Tus hijos te llaman.
¿Donde estás madre de mi alma?"

The Pain of a Mother

Who knows what there is within the heart?
Nobody in the world can see what you carry on the inside.
Anguish, desperation, yearning, scorn, deceit.
People only see in you what your exterior can reflect.
But it cannot reflect what your soul carries inside.
That pain that burns you, that oppresses you and breaks
your soul.
That pain that oozes as if it were a sore.
Yes, that burning pain that singes you like a flame
is the pain of a mother who suffers
because from the deepest part of her heart
there is a voice that says, "Your children are calling you.
Where are you mother of my soul?"

Yudelka
translated by Olga Candelario

Party Blowers

As I spoke to him, I felt the ease of the pressure on my chest,
the slight lessening of that ever-constant pain in my heart
and soul. It had been so long since we talked but today was
a very special day. Today is his birthday.

As we are talking I force back the tears while questioning
him regarding his birthday party that another woman was
fortunate enough to be a part of this year and not me.

He rambled on about all the excitement, the vast array of
foods, all his favorites of course. I see now that this other
woman is trying to gain a place in his heart, perhaps even
replace the piece of his heart that I hold.

This thought throws me into fear, even a little anger, but I stay quiet about it.

Then out of nowhere he says "Listen to this!" there is a pause, then the funny horn blow of a party blower. This catches me off guard, and we both laugh. He does it again, to make me laugh, and I do. I ask him if he received my gifts. He says yes. I ask him if he misses me as much as I miss him.

There is a yearlong silence, then he replies "When ya coming home Mom, I miss you so much." The pain is back in my heart, only worse now.

Patricia

FAMILY

You Dave

Just knowing that you are gone
And won't be there when I get out
Leaves me scared.
Who can I run to little brother?
You who always looked up to me
And you who I kissed the ground
You walked on, you David.
You Dave who when I was wrong
Said I was right
You Dave who wiped the tears when
I cried and cried with me
You Dave who hurt when I hurt
And always said it will be all right.
You Dave, who always said, *Don't
Leave me Sis!*
Now I'm saying it's you who left me
Dave, who can I run to?
Who's gonna say the
right things Dave said, Who?

Nerieda

As Much As I Can

I never had a closeness with my mother.
We can be friendly for a while,
short spans of time, separated
from my mother at a very young age
we grew distant. She feels more than I do.
She blames herself more than I do.
Wishing I loved her more,
wishing I felt love more.
Lack of feeling in my heart.
How can this have a good ending
with no good start?
There is a concern in the eyes as she looks on,
she tried to deal with me, tries to be strong.
She blames herself for the problems I have.
I don't blame her,
but I don't let her in.
Sometimes I wish she didn't feel so guilty,
Yet, I can't relieve her pain.
I feel no pain for things I should.
Pain is a feeling I lack,
but she feels all the time.
I love my mother as much as I can love.
It isn't much but it's all I have to give.
I appreciate when I feel again.
It's not often enough.

Barri

What I Save

I save old pictures, pieces of yarn,
old letters from my boyfriend and husband,
I save my girls' fallen-out teeth.
I save my son's hair and his hospital hat.
I save recipes and drawings.
I save all kinds of books and magazines.
I save the memories of my children's births.
I save memories of all the things I've done
with loved ones who have passed on.
I save the sound of raindrops falling on the roof.
I save the smell of the ocean and the sound
of the waves crashing along the rocks.
I save the many hopes and dreams
that some day I hope I will be able to fulfill.
I save all my mistakes from the past
and present in hopes to help me maintain
a better future for my family and myself.

Melissa

Memé

Sweet smells came
from your kitchen,
cookies pies and cakes,
all the little clothes
you made me
each stitch
filled with love.

Then one day
it happened,
Memé, you forgot
all that you did,
but it wasn't
your fault.

Memé one day
you got sick
your heart
beat no more
I'll never forget
your loving eyes
or tender touch.

God has you
now, Memé,
loving you
like I did.

Wendy

Grandmother

Grandmother, thank you for praying for me when I was a child. Thanks for being there for me. Thank you for accepting my phone calls every other day and for delivering my messages of the things I had to say. Thank you for helping my mother with me when I was getting out of hand and teaching me to learn from my mistakes that only you could understand.

Grandmother thank you for mothering me and taking my side when you always knew it was really my fault. Thank you for not blaming me for my parent's mistakes. Thank you for waking up in the middle of the night to bail me out of trouble and for teaching me to respect only those who respect me and love myself before another.

I thank both of you for giving me life cause if it weren't for you I wouldn't have been born for you are both one of the roots of my life. Thank you.

Lanisha

To My Sisters

You have stood by me,
have taken in my children
and loved them as your own.
Through my incarceration
you have kept me positive
and always told me to stay strong,
that no matter what, we are together
if only in spirit.

We have been through so much
in our life and we've remained close
and I just want to let you know

how much I appreciate
and how much I love you guys.
I thank God every night for you two
and tell him to keep you safe.
I'll be home soon and once again
there will be three not just two.

I love you.

Lissette

Daddy

Daddy, these are final words
        I always wanted to say to you
        but never got the chance.
Daddy, when I was a little girl,
        I used to go to sleep at night,
        dreaming of the day you would
        find me.

Daddy, I missed having you around when I was little. The
     longing grew as I grew up.
Daddy, they told me lies about
     you. Some so bad it
     made me cry, longing for the truth.
Daddy, as I grew up, becoming
     a young woman, being married
     with children of my own, I still
     thought about you and where you were.
Daddy, the day I got the message
     that my dad and mom were
     looking for me, I truly didn't
     know what to make of it.
Daddy, first thing is: Mom and
     me haven't spoken in
     a few years. I did not
     trust her. She has lied to me
     so many times.
Daddy, to us the only way
     to find out the truth was
     to drive back where I grew
     up and find her, because
     if I found her, you had to be close by.
Daddy, the minute I stepped out
     of the car I knew you were
     my dad; we looked so much alike.
Daddy, I was angry at you for not
     being there when I needed
     you the most—all through
     the years of abuse I endured.
Daddy, after I heard what you said
     and how it was Mom
     that separated us, I was filled
     with sorrow, because I got angry
     at the wrong person.

Daddy, you treated my like your
    little girl, even thought I was
    all grown up. It felt good.
Daddy, I know our time together
    was cut short due to terminal illness
    nor you or God could stop.
Daddy, the five years we spent
    together hold some wonderful
    memories and I will
    always remember the times
    we shared together.
Daddy, you are a wonderful
    grandfather. I could see
    what you meant to them by the sparkle
    in their eyes and their laughter.
Daddy, don't worry, when they get older,
    I'll share all the wonderful
    memories with them too.
Daddy, don't worry, I'll always
    be your little girl, your Cora Lee,
    no matter how old I get.
Daddy, remember I always love you.
Daddy, for now this is my only way
    to say goodbye to you, but when
    I come home, I'll find out where
    you rest in peace and no longer suffering,
    and there, I'll say my goodbyes, but
    you'll always remain alive in my heart and
    thoughts.
Daddy, I love you.

Cora

I Left My Momma Standing

I left my momma standing
Crying in the midnight sky.
As I ran down the rocky road.

I left my momma standing,
screaming my name to come back…
I heard her, but kept on running
Through the rocks as they dug into my feet.

I left my momma standing
Wondering where I was going, but I
believe deep in her heart she knew.

I left my momma standing
as she left me standing, too.

Lisa

Smells

When I read letters from my mother, I smell Florida. She lives in New Port Richey, so I think of cigarettes, Newports and can smell the tobacco. It's so nasty! I can smell the beaches, the salt water, I even hear people having a good time. I smell me down there with my best friend that I met down there before. I remember we used to play jokes on this little boy who lived across the street from us. We would go over and ring the doorbell or knock on the boy's window and run. Well one time I did that, and his father came out the front door with a shotgun. Oh boy I could smell the bullets just waiting inside. Thank God he didn't shoot any of us. I was scared to death.

Lisa

In This Picture

In this picture I was small hanging in the back yard at my aunt's cookout. There was plenty of food and drinks, people coming and saying hi and hugging each other cause they haven't seen each other in such a long time. Big smiles big hugs long talks about what's going on.

Please fix me a plate of that good smelling food that my mom and auntie had cooked just for the cookout: hot dogs and beans, potato salad, chips and chicken, and hamburgers. Oh, how I got full with drinks too! Pictures were taken to remind you of a good time. Smile! That's one for the book of pictures. You'll never forget the time at auntie's cookout. That was the Shit!

Patrice

I float on the water

I love to hear my birds sing
I believe in God
My daughter came to visit me from New York
I love my grandchildren

I am in peace with my friend Ruth
In the summer we see lots of bugs flying around
I am doing good in my recovery
When you cross the street you cross on the green light

I'm happy that I am sober today
I had a banana for lunch
I need to go to meetings more
I miss my father very much

I cannot forget my son
I heard my grandson cry
My mother had a cat called Kitty but she died
I am going to visit my friend Ruthie

I have a pair of pearl earrings
I saw the birth of my granddaughter
I love summer cause we go to lots of places
I say my prayers every night

I like to drink coffee
I love to lay on my pillow
I love those jeans she's wearing
I just had a death in my family

I have tears in my eyes when I speak of my son
I have to pick up his clothes
I am leaving soon to go to my house

I count the stars as I lie on my bed

My hands hurt when I write a lot
I have a feather pillow
I don't menstruate anymore
My grandson likes to hammer

I had a dream about my boyfriend
He has nice lips
I have faith in God
There was a bad storm in Florida

She wore a purple dress to graduation
The butterfly is in my room
I had a nice childhood
I love to work hard to save money

She shouts at me
He comforts me all the time
I blush when he kisses me
I float on the water.

Iris

Grandmother/Abuelita

Old lady/gray hair and old hands
Sweet person
The best food
The best consejos/advice
The best house
The best person in the world
The best listener
Gray hair and old hands
The sweet voice that I will never forget

My Grandmother, she was an old lady with a lot of gray hair. She was a sweet person. I can't forget the great food that she made for me, and I can't forget the best consejos (advice) she always gave to me. I always remember my grandmother's house; a small house, but beautiful. And I always remember that my grandmother never saw me because she lost her vision (vista) when she was so young. She was completely blind, but she was doing everything in her house. I always remember that she made the best food and always saved the food for me after school. I will always remember my grandmother. She was a good listening person and I will remember her because she and my mother are the best people for me in this world. My grandmother died about fifteen years ago, but I will always remember her. I still have her in my heart.

Carmen

Siarra

I still think of you almost everyday. You were a good friend, a good mother and a very good baby-sitter.

I still remember the very first day that you entered my home. Instantly it became OUR home. To the world you are a scary vicious dog, a pitbull, to be exact, but to me you are an angel—an angel that nobody will ever know as I know.

I was there throughout your three pregnancies that were never successful. I cried when you cried because you could not bear the pain any longer. I comforted you in good and bad times, just as you comforted me. And

now, my best friend, you Siarra, are gone—gone without even being able to say goodbye.

I miss you so much I can feel the pain in my soul. I miss your happy face and wagging tail at the sight of seeing me. If you were here I would tell you that you are a part of me, and

always will be my family. I am at ease knowing that my angel friend is with the rest of the angels. I will never forget you...

Allison

Forgotten

Have you forgotten me?
Someone so close?
Have you forgotten me, someone you love?
Have you forgotten me,
someone who was there for you?
Have you forgotten, my dear sister?
Where are you now when I need you the most?
Where are you now?
You've left me for dead,
You've left me to rot to death without a second thought.
How could you do that to me?
Have you forgotten me?
This seems to be sadly true.
Thus in the end, I've forgotten about you.
No more worries, no more tears,
to be forgotten is my biggest fear.
You've gone and made my fear come true,
but you know what?
To hell with you!

Sabrina

Mis Sitios Secretos

Cuando yo estoy de mal humor
o triste me voy a mi cuarto,
a mi cuarto a dibujar
cuando me siento triste.
En Puerto Rico me voy
a andar para los montes,
a la orilla del mar, al río a mirar
los peses brincar en el agua.

Y en el monte oigo
el zumbido del viento
que parece que me habla,
el rechinar de los árboles
que parecen que se hablan.
Ahí estoy casi todo el día
y el cantido de los pichones
y ahí me paso casi todo el día.

También me gusta jugar
con las olas del mar que van
y vienen los marullos.
Recojo caracoles y escribo
en la arena mis pensamientos
para que las olas se los lleve.
Ahora me hace falta todo eso,
por que es muy bonito.

El mar, el río, el monte,
son mis mejores amigos.
Ellos me oyen
y no se lo dicen a nadie.
Ellos me aconsejan
en su suave lenguaje.

My Secret Places

When I am in a bad mood
or sad I go away to my room,
to my room to draw
when I feel sad.
In Puerto Rico I go for a walk
in the hills, to the seaside,
the river, to watch the fish
jump in the water.

And in the hills I hear
the humming of the wind
that seems as if it speaks to me,
the squeaking of the trees
that seem to speak to each other.
I am there almost all day
with the singing of the birds.
I spend almost all day that way.

I also like to play
with the waves of the sea
that ebb and flow in swirls.
I gather seashells and write
my thoughts in the sand
so that the waves can take them away.
Now I miss all of that.

The sea, the river, the hills,
are my best friends.
They listen to me and they
don't repeat it to anybody.
They advise me
in their own soft language.

Santos
translated by Olga Candelario

Ponce, Puerto Rico
--after George Ella Lyon

I come from red and black colors,
From the great Cathedral church,
From the most ancient fire station in history.
I come from where you can hear the scream of Vieques
up close,
From the most beautiful sky and ancient streets.
I come from laughter, guitars and guiros,
From where The Victory Lions roar
and the people are more humble and well known.
I still remember the smell of the sugar cane
From where they distill Seralles rum.
I come from ancient castles,
And legends that scared me when I was young.
I come from great statues
That in my adolescence I profaned,
From the fountain in the plaza which I dressed
As a bride with a bottle of Vel dish soap.
I come from where the stars are most beautiful,
The weather most agreeable, the people less hypocrites.
I come from where living is an art.
I come from Ponce, Puerto Rico.

Jackie

Perfume

White Diamonds, Diamonds and Emeralds, Liz Taylor, Ralph
Lauren

These are the scents that I miss

Tommy Girl, Nautica, J Lo

This is what I want to smell like when I walk out the door.

Victoria Secret, Dreamers

Behind the ear, on the wrist, on the neck, behind the knees

Splash on, spray on, Sprinkle here, mist there. Bathe in

Oh, you smell so good, a breath of sweet smells

I miss you so much

JoAnn

Mississippi

I was born in Mississippi. I walked through the mud bare foot. I am black that I am. My daddy chopped cotton and so did my momma. My parents made sure we had food on the table and clothes on our back and shoes on our feet. Oh yeah my daddy drank his liquor straight or should I say he drank his moonshine straight—boy did he ever, but when I think back on the days when I was growing up in Mississippi as I often do we didn't have the best of everything. It didn't matter what we had because we had the most valuable thing in life which was momma and daddy teaching us how to be strong, always keep your head up through good and bad times but most of all keep love in your heart and a smile on your face. I am still the same old black girl with the same old blues.

Deborah

Where I'm From
--after George Ella Lyon

I'm from Never sees.
I'm from taking your tongue on a sleigh ride.
I'm from warm chocolate chip cookies
and a roast in the oven,
from the subway, the el and looking out the window.
I'm from touch football on a hot summer night
from Alvida and Robina gossiping at the head of the table.
I'm from getting stuck in the woods
and following the horse back home in the dark.
I'm from hand-me-downs and suburbs,
from killdeer crying away their nests
and *I can't believe he ate the whole thing.*
I'm from the clean plate club and
But I did the dishes last *night!*
I'm from secretary and construction
from the sunset over the pool
and ice cream dripping out of my hand.
I'm from jumping out of my dad's truck,
from playing marbles to sliding
from cleaning out the garden and
taking the rotten vegetables to the truck.
I'm from all of these good moments
and good memories.

Michele, Kathy, Jackie, Daryl, Donna, Myrna, Kitty, and Johanna

It's a One Way Street

One way street meaning going in one

direction only. No going the opposite way. Continue,

do not look back, we walk past the green grass

but only to notice trash on the other side where

the prostitutes roam streets, junkies in

the alleyway using puddles of water to put

in their syringes, drug dealers stand on the

corner selling nothing but change, chump

40's and 8 balls. Little children chasing after

the ice cream truck but the melody fades

away as gun shot sounds come to focus,

the rap music is over blared by sirens,

the basket ball on the court stops bouncing

and the children on the swings stop

swinging. A homeless man on the sidewalk

holding a dirty Dunkin' Donuts cup

asking for quarters. Next to him lays an

empty bottle. There's shattered glass on the

pavement from someone's car being smashed

with a brick, but what about the children

playing with bare feet? —But we keep

going, keep going, it's a one way street,

thinking at the end of it there will be

a pretty neighborhood, but nah, man, it

continues, so forget the one way street,

don't matter if it's two way or not

for the same is recurring.

I ask the question, who knows about a one way street?

Stacy

You Must Be Quick

You must be quick to light the cigarette

for the flame only lasts so long.

She cooks Mexican food on this stove, which from

any other Mexican it would most likely taste

right, but from her it is mush—no one wants

to eat her cooking. She cooks and leaves it

there for days. The stove with the

flame disgusts me. Young I am but

trying to cook, for I can't stand to taste

it no more. She reaches for the

bag of rice in the cabinet to pour

in the pan on the stove. Why is

this place cockroach infested? Why is

it I clean all the time and the foster mother

is a complete slob? The plaster from the walls crumbles

as well as does my life. I sit in the kitchen

with the flame on the stove going

—there's no heat. Here is the milk which

stays in cups on the kitchen floor for

the little roaches to climb into and

drown. I get up in the middle

of the night to go pee but

I must go past the kitchen…oops, I spill

the cups of milk and dirty the floor

but it ain't nothing, for the floor

is already dirty as well as this woman

who screams at me in a language

that is blank to me.

The kitchen used to be the worst place.

Take-out became a daily thing.

As for the milk, it's always sour.

And who cares if the flame goes

out on the stove—for my cigarette

I now have a lighter.

Stacy

High Yellas

--after George Ella Lyon

I am from the skipped generation of high
yellas and rough feet.
I am from snapping peas, picking strawberries
and peach trees,
farmhouses with little chicks: newborns
raped of life 'cause they end up
on my plate.
I am from Sunday School, bible verse
and choir rehearsals on Saturday,
Mary Janes & pig's feet.

I am from broken hearts of love
lost trying to mend again,
from one day I'll be back again
I am from Grandmothers,
foundations, "Mother May I"
and sneaking shots of corn liquor
and Michelob.
I am from long walks alone with tears
in my eyes, from falling every time
I rise.

Tracey

LOVE & VIOLENCE

My Deadly Dare

My skull will remain
Full of imprints
Of your sharp teeth.
It's sad but I just wanted
To see what's underneath.
Do you hurt just like me?
I felt all your teeth.

Lightening made you run away.
I should never have stayed
All I wanted was a hug,
But now I am dead
And you ran away.
I couldn't make you stay.
Only bone, I lay.

Marisol

Dirt

It's amazing how you have such talent.
Talent to make me feel like dirt.
Your words are more powerful
than you think—or maybe you know,
and I find
your words ringing in my head.
Now I'm not my own.
I just wish I was dead.
Cover me with the dirt.
You know, the dirt you make me feel like every day.
Just kick me around.
Dirt belongs on the ground anyway.
I am not your possession
though you act as if I am.
I'm trying to get away,
Make my way through the dirt
that I am buried in now.

Jessica

In My Face

I've always been very independent.
firm that I wanted a relationship
that was loving, caring,
and equal.
I thought finally here's
someone to spend
the rest of my life with.

It lasted nine months
or took me that long to get out of.

I never saw the control
getting dropped off
and picked up from work,
never being able to go to the store alone,
hardly ever talking to my friends,
never getting together on the weekends

friends call saying
he was taking me up too much

Arguments started
me wanting some time along
a shove here a push there.

Realizing my relationship with
my daughter was at risk
I got out. I had gone from wanting
a loving, caring, and sharing relationship
to betraying myself.

Why could everyone else see it but me?

Daryl

How Could You

What I meant to say was, how could you

rip my heart in two? How could I let you?

What I meant to say was, how could you

do what you've done?

What I meant to say was,

how should I treat you today?

What I meant to say was, you had no right.

What I meant to say was,

you better stay out of sight.

What I meant to say was, you better run

with all your might. What I meant to say was,

because you hurt my little girl, you will pay.

What I meant to say was

how could this have happened to my baby girl?

What I meant to say was, where the hell

was I when this happened? What I have been asking is,

how could I have let this happen?

What I have been asking is,

how could I have stopped this from happening?

What I have been asking is, what will I do

about all the pain she went through?

What will I do with all the pain I went through?

All the pain we are all going through?

How first and foremost can I forgive myself?

How?

Sabrina

I Ain't No Woman

Excuse me!
What did you say?
How dare you speak
to me in that way?
I ain't no woman,
is *that* what you say?
I'll have you know
I'm a woman everyday...
I cooked, I cleaned,
even sung your legacy,
gave everything up,
even being just me.
I did what I did
yes, I made my choice
so don't you dare look at me
in that tone of voice.
Did you think
without you I was nothing?
Well, surprise, surprise,
I am very much something.
I walk through this world
with such a desire,
my passion so strong
I can set you on fire.
You think to yourself
that you are so wild.
But in everyone's eyes
you're nothing but a child.
I ain't no woman,
that's what you think,
but that's not the case
after you have your third drink.
Remember the moon in my eyes, the

softness of my hair,
the speakings of love
and of how much you care.
If you want to leave
go ahead cause I'll guarantee,
you will never find
another woman like me.
Oh, I *am* woman,
of that you can be sure,
my mind is strong
and my heart is pure.
If you every try
to hurt me again,
you'd better be gone
by the time I count ten.
I'll kick your ass
from one room to another!
You are not my father
and I'm not my mother.
Oh yes, I am woman
and at times don't fight fair.
So, remember who I am
and remember, of me
you'd better BEWARE!

Veronica

Jose Is My Weakness

You are my weakness. Yes!
Don't look away like I'm not speaking to you.
Every time you look at me my heart rate
goes soaring, my knees become jelly
and my stomach has a million butterflies.
I become weak every time our bodies touch.
When I smell your scent in the air,
my body starts to tingle and ache for you.
Just seeing your sexy strut like you have
no care in the world makes me swoon.
I always want to reach out and touch you.
You make me weak in places
I never knew could become weak.
I want to hold you close to me
for an eternity and then some.
I want for you to always be mine.
You are my weakness and I never want
to be strong when it comes to you.
I have no shame and there is no cure
when it comes to how weak I am for you.

Lissette

Foolish Things

I've done foolish things for love and attention. How could I not do these things when he's telling me he loves me, that I'm his whole world, and he's wining and dining me? Then one day, out of the blue he says to me, "Babe I think we need to slow this down," cause he don't think it's gonna work out???

So we split but we might as well have stayed together cause every time he turned around I was there! I was playing security guard at his home, always watching out what was going on. I would go by his job just to see if he was there.

I found myself going to clubs even though I am not a club person, knowing that's where he'll be. I even called out my own name in clubs, "Deborah!" just to get his attention to make sure he remembered me. I would even play private investigator sneaking around in the bushes peeking in his windows to see who's in the house with him.

But, I'm over that now. I'm just remembering the foolish things I've done for LOVE.

Deborah

Cool Waters

When I smell Cool Waters, the cologne for men, it takes me back to when I first met my baby's daddy. He was about five foot nine, a hundred and eighty pounds, dressed all in black, brown skin and attractive. His haircut was freshly trimmed, and he was clean shaven. He had the most beautiful smile.

My baby's father and I were sitting on the porch talking about how come I always look evil and then we started talking about him and his job. We must have talked

for house and the next thing I know he was outlining my face
with his finger tip. Oh I like that and I didn't stop him. Then
he leaned over and kissed me I didn't stop that either, but we
are no longer together cause his Cool Waters cologne
grabbed the attention of someone else while I was gone.
Now when I smell Cool Waters I want to do something ugly,
but I can't 'cause he is my baby's daddy. Thanks a lot Cool
Waters.

Deborah

He Said

He said everything would be better than before.
He said that he would take good care of me,
make me a better person by being there for me.
He said he would try to fulfill my life with special
wishes and dreams to make them come true.
He said he would treat me like a queen of his heart.
He said he wouldn't ever depart.
He said he would be with me
for the rest of my life.
That's what he *said*.

Patrice

The Secret Lover

My eyes want to kiss your face.

I have no power over my eyes.

I just want to kiss your face.

I flow towards you out of my eyes,

a fine heat trembles over your shoulders,

it slowly dissolves your contours.

You are now with me, your body

powerless. Our eyes want each other.

We sit with our hands in our laps.

I shouldn't touch you, and same with you.

But my eyes kiss your face, your face

kisses my eyes. We rise out of ourselves

and no one can stop us. We flow

out and we're invisible, we can't

stop this unfathomable flowing,

this dazzle that knows neither end

nor beginning—but when at last

we turn our eyes toward each other

they are unaware, questioning, strangers'

eyes. I sink myself back into

your hands, you take up my

place under my eyelids.

Lisa

My Hips

My hips, these hips are a passion,
They move to their own beat as if there was
an orchestra inside my jeans,
These hips, my hips,
That I see looking back at me in the reflection

of my long full-length mirror.
They talk to me,
They empower me,
They tell me the secrets of my Baby's heart,
And school me on how to get the techniques right.

My hips, these big old hips that I have
are here and here to stay.
They are accompanied by my pretty bow legs
And the two of them are unstoppable.
I've used my hips to seductively lure
my prey into my spider's web,
And left him there as if I was saving him
for my midnight's snack,
He then showered me with his undivided attention
and he hung on my every word,
And the result of all this has him fallen
completely and utterly in love with me.
How you say…with these big Ol' hips?

Tashia

I Am

I am not one.
I am both.
I am your wife
and your mistress
I will clean your house
just to litter it with our clothes
I will make the bed
just to keep it wrinkled
I will wash and send the kids
to school just to make more
I will cook the food for you to eat
from my thighs
I will wash your clothes
just to see them on the floor
I will wash the floor
just to keep our sweat on it
I will spend hours dressing
just to spend minutes taking it all off
And I will love
just to be loved

Melissa

Magic

I was sentenced to 18 months in hell.
I used the time wisely, worked on a spell.
I found some pink paper
which is the color of love
and evoked the great spirits
that come from above.
I sent gifts to all elements
water, earth, fire and air.
I sacrificed to the spirits
a tiny braid of my hair,
poked holes in some apples
and used their natural smell
because candles and incense
weren't allowed in my cell.
I made crumbled leaves circle
then stood in my place,
cleared my mind, closed my eyes
and pictured your face.
It was the end of February
and the moon full and strong.
I started to dance
and chant a little song.
"One to seek him,
one to find him,
one to bring him,
one to bind him,
heart to heart forever one.
So say I, this spell is done."
I folded the pink paper,
and drew blood from a scar,
dripped my blood on the paper
in the design of a star.
Then I had to wait for the rising sun

of the next full moon to appear.
On that March morning,
sure enough, you were there.
The gods did enough.
The rest is up to me.
I can keep you in my heart,
or choose to set you free.
Something went wrong
and I think you should know.
My spell worked too well
'cause I can't let you go.

Joanna

Let's Talk

Startled by your silhouette
Controlled by your wicked eyes
Pivoting on your empty words
Accepting your lies
Hand feeding your ego without true thought
Secretly regretting your existence
Fighting for change
Understanding that joy will never show up
Knowing it's time to leave
Let's talk

Sonia

Golden Yellow

Golden yellow, fit for a girl not a fellow.
For me it is brought to show one's love,
Or one's delight.
My leg's a glistening brown, other girls frown.
Golden yellow not made for a fellow,
So I'll let the wind blow,
And rain fall
And kiss good night my golden yellow flowers.

Pennie

I Love You to Death

We meet, we talk.
We talk and talk, then decide
        to go out sometime.
He calls me, we set a date.
We go out on our date.
We have a blast, get along great!
We keep going out, I guess they
        call it going steady.
We do this steady thing for about a year.
We fall in love!
We get married.
He starts to hit me.
I still love him.
He starts cheating, he apologizes.
Of course I accept his apology.
I still love him.
He continues hitting me.
I love him, he's my husband.
He starts using alcohol and drugs,
I love him even more, I did this to him.

The beatings get worse,
I end up in the hospital.
I still love him.
I ask him, *"Please stop, lets*
    go get help. I am willing to go
    every inch of the way with you!"
He says, *"Bitch, you're the one who has the problem."*
I think for a moment, I agree.
Oh, how I love him.
Another year goes by.
The drinking and drugging have gotten worse.
The beatings are way out of control.
I am a prisoner in my own home. I don't ask this time,
I tell him that he goes and gets help or I'm leaving.
Oh, how I love him!
He beats me to a pulp.
I spend three and a half weeks in the hospital.
Yes, of course I still love him!
As I am driving myself home from
    the hospital, I stop and buy a gun.
Everything is great for about two weeks.
I love him. We even make love.
He goes out one night.
He comes home messed up!
He comes towards me with that look in his eyes!
As I say, *"I love you,"* a tear
fills my right eye.
He comes closer and starts raising his arms.
I love him!
I grasp the gun!
God, I love him!
I point it at him.
"I love you!" I shout!
He takes another step.
Doesn't he know I love him?

He says, *"Ah, you stupid bitch, you're in*
    love with me so damn much that you
    could never pull the trigger."
I love him more than life!
He lunges at me.
I pull the trigger.
A shot is fired.
Dear God, I love him.
I dial 911.
I love him.
I place the gun down next to him.
I sit down in the chair
shaking from head to toe.
I love him.
The police and medical team show up.
They tell me that he is dead.
I love him.
I am locked behind bars now and
I think about him from time to time.

Melanie

Seashells

Salt water over my feet
Seashells in my sad hands
It is hunger I taste in the breeze…
Shades of night are
Falling fast as the blue glass sea
becomes a tuneless treble to my ears.
I am lost in the absence of sound.
I no longer understand the logic of words.
Visions of days depart into the sea
like seashells adrift on the sand.
Once lost, Once found.

Toni

I Get Angry When

I get angry when
I try to listen but cannot hear,
say or ask something and get no response.
I get angry when
I fail to see something right before my eyes
or read into something far too much.
I get angry when
I fail at something that I know I should
be able to succeed at.
I get angry at myself for not even trying
at something for fear of failing.

Jennifer

I Used to Be

I used to be a spoiled brat.
I used to be a little sister,
with pig tails and ribbons.
I used to be a dancer,
dancing my way to fame.
I used to be a windmill
blowing in the wind.
I used to be a door
allowing pain to come in.
I used to be happy,
and always smiling
bright as the sun.
I used to be so many things
in my own private thoughts
of what I really want to be,
but now I am really happy
because I can be me.

Tina

I Would Like You to Know

I would like you to know that this is not what I dreamed
my life would be when I was a little girl lying in bed
with my big sister next to me, talking and wishing
about the perfect life and perfect husbands.
I would like you to know that my two daughters
are my greatest accomplishments,
that they are the reason for my existence.
I would like you to know that my mom
is the greatest woman in the world and that
she always taught me right from wrong,
but I didn't listen, that she is strong and beautiful
and that I pray to God to be like her someday.
I would like you to know that I am part of a trio
that includes me and my two sisters
that when we are all together we are indestructible.
Together we have made the best of everything
and always stand by each other no matter what;
that my two sisters are my left and my right!
I would like you to know that today
my life has a direction and hope;
that I have evolved into someone
I dreamed of being.

Lissette

We Would Like You To Know

We would like you to know
not everything is black and white.
Not everything goes in perfect harmony.
Not everyone can sing in a choir.
We would like you to know
not all of us can be good mothers.
Not all of us have good childhoods.
Not all of us get good grades.
Not all have brothers or sisters.
We would like you to know
not all of us are drug addicts or drug-pushers.
Not all of us are thieves.
Not all of us have positive thoughts.
Most of us have negative thoughts.
As to why we do, it's like trying to explain
Mother Nature, and why the sky is blue.
We would like you to know we are all different,
with different personalities and backgrounds,
different languages and races,
but we all learn that unforgettable phrase
that all cultures know or signal—
It's either sticking a middle finger up
when driving or the favorite words "fuck you!"
We would like you to know that we
are all made by the same God
but He let us all choose to be different.

Jackie

Through My Window

At night before I lie down I always look
through the little window in my room
and I can see the fresh breeze that travels around the world.
I look too at the sky full of stars that invite me
to play in the game of happiness with them.
It's so different to see how things
look from my little window.

Everything looks alive as if all those
things that really do not die suddenly regain
life, even if it were only for my eyes.
It reminds me of my dreams
in which the unreal, the mystical and the forbidden
come together as if all of them were normal.

In these moments of cruel loneliness
that I'm living in this cemetery
that they call prison, my little window
is my guide, is my company because it is
the one who makes me keep in mind that some day
I will have a tomorrow in which
this sadness ends and my soul blossoms.

Yudelka
translated by Olga Candelario

I Don't Have To...

I don't have to sit here with my eyes wide open,
not seeing things clearly.
I don't have to pray and hope I'll be out of here soon,
my hopes rise as far as I allow them to, even reaching the
sky.
I don't have to dream of being free and out
or how I'm going to say *goodbye* or *see you later*.
I don't have to put myself through this pain and cry silent
tears or scream heavy tears while they fall like rain.
I don't have to fear being along while leaving here.
I don't have to ask who loves me or really cares.
Or if they're going through what I'm going through
in this pain.
I know some will be there, some will not.
Because the ones that won't be there at the end, I don't need.
I'll close my eyes and open my heart.
I'll pray and hope for all the good and the new life I'll take on
when I walk out this door alone to fight the battle
I've yet to win,
the one I'll conquer at the end.
I don't have to do this alone.

Lisa

Woman

I am a woman, a Black woman that is,
Strong & independent, woman with class
That's what type of woman I am,
some who don't know me may not agree
but they can kiss my ass.
There are many different types of women,
but I'm not like many women,
and I'm not just any woman,
I'm a respectful Black woman
who gives and gets respect,
beautiful,
loving,
active,
confident,
kind.
That could be any woman,
that could be many women,
but I'm talking about one woman.
That woman is me.

Lanisha

I'm Me!

   If I have to go through something so terrible to lose weight and not feel good about it or myself, I'd rather stay plus size and feel great inside and out continuing to smile. Any my health is excellent, so there for Slimfast!
   Jenny Craig, you can move over 'cause I'm sitting down to eat. Pass me them pork chops, and sweet potatoes 'cause this is who I am. I'm Me!

Deborah

102

Myself

I am shadowed in a living purgatory. Control is thick like smoke. It's so heavy, but I'll never grasp it. My Faith is being tortured blindly, near annihilation. It is dark where I am and it's been long since hope has found its way firmly into my heart.

I look toward epic and mystical delusion and maybe a light will come through and shine because I am now in my darkest hour. The essence of time deceives me and betrays my heart.

Alone, I am with a thousand others. I smile like I know a secret that no one else will ever know and I barely hold but obtains everyone's morbid curiosity and endless fascination.

And if you look very closely at the shadow that is surrounding me, suffocating my vision like smog, you will see I am solid concrete underneath. You will see the shadow is the final ingredient to my ultimate completion as a human being. A strong unbreakable desire that others will long to have.

God's will is a test I never anticipated to endure, a test that have become my own. Suffering has become my favorite friend. So I do know a secret that I refuse to share. A secret that is learned better on its own. Determination, desire, sacrifice and light. Yet life is beautiful and I will not be broken.

Lisa Q.

ME

I am always student and sometimes teacher. I am here to scatter pieces of me around your conscience, an offering from my singed soul to all of humankind. Learn, learn, grow, and know me. I am the one for whom you lacked compassion. I am the one you turned from in disgust. Now something draws you to me. You can't look away. I am strength. I am example. I am fragmented but no longer "broken." I serve as reminder that we, you, are divine and noble. I live to acknowledge depravity and lack and to name these things. I don't turn away. I accept. I offer hope. I provide the lesson from having lived and survived. I found power through my experience. I was fear, now I am courage. Find me. Gain understanding. Find me. Education your heart. Find me. Seek change.

Dede

Little Black White Girl

Little black white girl
I know what it means
not everything is
quite how it seems

Too light to be Black
too dark to be white
growing up in this world
was a hell of a fight

You don't fit in
to any particular clique
and trying to
just makes you sick

When hate would arise
and people would fight
they always wanted to know
Do you fight for black or white

It wasn't hard to answer
Hmm Let me see
I'll just cut myself in half
and I'll fight with just me!

People would finally
begin to understand
no matter what color I am
I have a right to live on this land

they say of color
I am of two
well I say one
so what you going to do

Little Black white girl
Just struggling to be free
For the only one I have to free
is myself, yes, just me.

Veronica

In the Midst of This Wreckage

In the midst of this wreckage called life
I struggle to find myself.
Daughter, sister, mother, wife,
I struggle to find myself.
Different cultures, religions and traditions,
I struggle to find myself.
Coming out of the womb, losing all inhibitions,
I struggle to find myself.
In closets, under beds, turning over every rock,
I struggle to find myself.
Years of failures and achievements,
Happiness, sadness and pain,
Grey skies, sun-filled mornings,
All the beauty that comes with the rain...
Then comes the guilt, shame and abuse.
I struggle.
I build the walls higher because what's the use.
I'm tired of struggling.

Heather

Blackest vs. Brightness

Once in the blackest night
I was hollow, carved out like a pumpkin
having no feelings or a will to care.
I didn't know myself, nor did I care to.
I didn't know you or your friend.
I didn't even know my family.
Once in the blackest of night,
I was scared and lonely,
fearing what would take away

106

my craving to be satisfied,
not to remember the punch of that fist,
the slap of that hand,
the penis of that rape,
the rhythm of that flesh beating up on mine.
Once in the blackest of night
I inhaled smoke that made me forget,
forget the beginning of every bad new day—
a day that could've been good if I gave it a chance.
Once in the blackest of night,
I fell to my knees,
tired of chasing to find me,
who I really am.
Once in the blackest of night
I gave up and surrendered,
begging to be free and whole.
It all began in a cell that trapped me in.
Once in the blackest of night
I lay praying to be new.
Once lost but now I'm found,
from the blackest of nights to the brightness of day.

Lisa

Dust and Ashes
--after George Ella Lyon

I am from the Alley,
dirt roads an' collard greens.
I am from the Sixties, Woodstock,
Afros and Free Love
where there was no love.
I am from confusion
and racism with no identity.

I am reborn.
I am from ashes
I am from dust.
I am from tomorrow. I am
a torch in the dark.
I am from valley lows
and mountain highs,
I am from Light.
I am from the four corners of the earth.
I am from the mountaintop
and I am Good News.

Loren

Certain Paths

We would like you to know that we, the women,
have chosen certain paths in our lives
that have taken most of us to this point
where you nor I would like to live inside
where the blood and veins reside,
because of all the struggles
that have come between me and I.

Dorinda

Cold Streets

Sitting here contemplating
on what awaits me out in the streets
Cold it be, the beats that I used to do,
or just school that my crew considers for fools.
Nah. I'm a do the 360
and just see how this new life fits me
and if it's fa me
Then by all means
I'm the new leader of that new crew
that no one thought was possible
to be or even destined to be.
So here I start by trying
to express my new creativity.
If I don't speak I'll never be heard
and if I don't express with my left,
It will never be read.

Dorinda

I've Learned

I've learned that nothing worth having
comes without a price;
that not all the criminals in the world
are locked-up in jails
(some of them have the keep);
That I would rather live alone
than to shack-up with someone
I don't really know;
and that my greatest test in life
is one I've been allowed to take
over again until I get it right.

Moana

Bike Ride
--After Laura Kasischke

Who knew then some day
I would stand up again
Those boys would still be
Waiting out side the Stop n Go
Cigarettes growing older
I got a chance to live life
And just to be able to
Wipe the crumbs off the
Kitchen table with a sponge
Remembering them thinking
What I have been given or what
I missed.

Awilda

Begging the Devil

No need to look outside to see that there's
No sun shining.
No sun shining, shining.
I can't get up, I can't get free, I can't break,
Break out. I can't break out of these walls I construct.
No prison worse, worse than the one
I build my own damn self.

My head keeps tumbling, tumbling, tumbling
Down upon the ground. No way to stop it,
There's no cease fire, no reprieve, there's no
Escaping, no escaping, no escaping me.

They call it bi-polar/manic depressive, anxiety
Borderline, ADD, OOOH, ICT.
Please release me, can't you see me...

Can't you see me, cant' you set me free.
I swear, I promise, I guarantee, this time
It ain't no lie. I beg the devil to post my bond,
I beg God to keep me clean.
Need to remember, I gotta wanna, want it to be.

What's done in the dark comes out in the light,
Except for the lies on Capitol Hill.
This is truth, this is justice, this is the American way.
Better pack it up, grab you baggage,
The damage has already been done,
No I ain't gonna love it.

Kelly

So Kissy-Kissy

So kissy-kissy and so sharky
No better way to describe her
Soft lips caressing the back of my neck
While my toes dangle above murky water

That girlish laugh
Behind devilish grins
That sensual stare
She always wins

Your best friend and enemy
Swimming together as one
Stay secure on your raft
Her game's already begun
There's no way to tell day to day
What to expect or when
Just be ready to play rough
And know some tears you can't mend

She's sneaky, she's fast, she comes from behind
And I just can't resist
The chase is on so beware of the fin
Lurking in the thick, heavy mist.

Heather

A Different Place

I am from another world
A different place.

I am from the earth as in solid ground
Roaming here and there
Roaming almost anywhere
Yet can't sit still for long.

I am from the air, light breeze, forceful winds.
Like God's kiss and baby's breath
Standing tall, won't be blown down.

I am from fire, bold, hot.
Strong.
Burning bright through night and light,
Consuming all that's in its path,
Fearful to burn out.

I am from water, flowing, cool, running
Sweet. Rushing force filled with life yet
Allowing calm still and deep.

Kelly

Second Chance Lord

I've learned that life sometimes gives you a second chance because it wasn't very long ago that I could have been doing a twenty-five year prison sentence after wrapping up in three years. It wasn't very long that I was out before relapsing, only 'cuz I didn't change people, places, and things. "I'm strong. I can handle anything." No No NO! Not strong enough 'cuz here I am on another two and a half. Lucky was I? I'd say so seeing I had four year's probation with twenty-five suspended.

I guess that's what happens when you dance with the devil too long. I was in love with that bastard. But there are times I must say I'd like to go out dancing with him but that thought only lasts a few moments and I brush him off my shoulder and on to the floor. I step on him and walk all over him just like he did to me for years.

I reach my hands out to the beauty of the Lord. He walks with me every day and holds my hand. I dance with my lord and raise my hand high pulling him down from the glorious sky. He washes me new daily. I see my ex-love, the devil every day. He is in all forms. But my new love from above, I see him also. I saw a sparrow while Mo, Ruth, and I were doing bible twelve step work. That's when I felt him. I got chills, when I laid my eyes on that sparrow.

I love you Lord. I've set my body free Lord, it's yours. Hide me under the wing of your angels and protect me from all evil and the Shadows of death. Keep me afloat upon my new walk with you.

Lisa

Hablando Con Mi Espiritud

Hoy camino de la mano con mi espiritu y en un momento de desesperación quise preguntarle ¿Por que se sufre tanto en esta vida? Él quedó en un absoluto silencio que a mi me pareció una eternidad, pero, luego de un largo suspiro, me contestó. Se sufre, por que casi siempre escogemos cosas equivocadas. Escogemos Parejas equivocadas y hacemos decisiones equivocadas. Luego le pregunté ¿Qué debería hacer yo para tener un poco de Felicidad? Esta vez contestó con más rapidez que la primera vez, y me dijo; cada vez que vallas a tomar una decisión en tu vida detente y piensa ¿A Dios le agrada? ¿Le hace bien o mal a mi vida y a mi alma? Recuerda siempre, yo soy tu mejor amiga y deseo lo mejor para ti. Por eso cada vez que tomas una decisión incorrecta soy la que susurra a tu oído como un leve sonido, ¡no por Favor no lo hagas! Eso te traerá malas Consecuencias así que pon más atención y une tus Sentimientos y tus emociones a lo que es real y verdadero y te aseguro que desde ese momento en adelante las dos dejaremos de sufrir.

Talking To My Spirit

Today I walk hand in hand with my spiritually and in a moment of desperation ask, "Why is there so much suffering in this life?"

She remained in absolute silence for what seemed to me like an eternity, but after a long sigh she answered me. "There is suffering because almost always we choose the wrong things. We choose the wrong partners and we chose the wrong things."

Later I asked her, "What can I do to be able to have a little bit of happiness?"

This time she answered a bit quicker than the first time, and said to me, "Each time you have to make a decision in your life, stop and think: Would it please God? Will it do good or ill to my life and soul? Remember always, I am your best friend and I wish the best for you, that is why each time you make a wrong decision I am the one who whispers lightly in your ear, No! Please don't do it! This will bring you bad consequences so pay more attention and unite your feelings and your emotions to what is real and true and I assure you that from that moment forward, we will both stop suffering."

Yudelka
translated by Olga Candelario

Declaration of Independence

Hoy he sentido como sí el mundo
se hubiera venido abajo es una sensación
que no puedo describir, algo que te quema
y te atrapa por dentro como si estuvieras
en un laberinto sin salida.
Hoy me he sentido acorralada sin sonido
con la necesidad de un niño que necesita
el calor de unos brazo tibios, unos brazos
que le enseñen el camino debido.
Hoy he querido correr y volar como
gaviota sin nido, traspasar ese horizonte
que ante mis ojos esta escondido.
Hoy siento que muero o quizás que vivo
pero vivo en un valle de sombra, como sí
fuera un cementerio de almas sin abrigo.
Pero hoy quiero darme declaración de independencia
y gritar a los cuatros vientos que aunque
pudieron encancelar mi cuerpo, no pueden,
ni podrán encarcelar mi alma y mi espiritud.

Declaration of Independence

Today I have felt as if the world had come down.
It's a sensation that I cannot describe,
something that burns you and it catches you
on the inside as if you were in a labyrinth without exit.
Today I have felt cornered without sound, with the need
of a child who needs the warmth of arms, arms that teach the
correct path.
Today I have wanted to run and to fly like a gull without a
nest, to go past that horizon that is hidden before my eyes.
Today I feel that I could die or maybe I could live, but live in
the valley of shadows, as if it were a cemetery of souls
without shelter.
But today I want to make a declaration of independence and
to shout to the four winds that although they were able to jail
my body, they could not, nor will they be able to jail my soul
and my spirit.

Yudelka
translated by Olga Candelario

Perdoname

Perdoname, Senor, Perdoname por no perdonar cuantas
veces te he pedido perdo n. Quizas mas de 1,000 vecse al dia.

Que hipocrita fui, podiendote que me perdonaras cuanto yo
necesitabas. Perdonar primero que egocentricos.

Somos muchas veces los seres humanos nos creemos dioses.
Nos creemos perfecto cuando lo que estamos es podrido por
dentro. El se humano ha puesto sus mismos reglas,
Personame senor por yo haber puesto antes las mias.

Ahora senor quiero que seas tu quien dirijas mi vida.
Guiame con tu santo espiritu, senor y si te fallo una vez mas
por favor.

Perdoname otra vez.

Guiame con tu santo espiritu, senor y si te fallo una vez mas
por favor.

Perdoname otra vez.

Forgive Me

Forgive me God.
Forgive me for not being forgiving.
How many times have I asked you
For forgiveness,
Maybe a thousand times a day.

What a hypocrite!
I have been asking you to forgive me

When I had not learned
To forgive others.

What an ego!
There are a lot of times
That we humans think we are Gods.
We think we are perfect
When we are rotting inside.

We humans have made our own rules.
Forgive me God
For trying to make my own.
Now, my Lord,
I want you to direct my life
With your Holy Spirit.

Lord, if I fail you once again,
Forgive me.

Yudelka
translated by Olga Candelario

Freedom

Society's cruel intentions lay,
to slaughter the poor while the rich get away,
Do your time in prisons, walls so cold,
once vivid with life strong and bold.
Now, who do I call when all is in despair?
I once heard someone say, *Try Jesus, he'll be there.*
I tried to remember the "Our Father's" prayer,
but all I could think of was—would he really care?
I went to church once on Easter, prayed before meals
—wait, okay, once before supper.
Everything I've been through I try to recall,

where was Jesus before I made this great fall?
I mean, I almost died several times,
lost all I had, even my mind,
on one's shoulder I never had,
just me, my pride and several brown bags.
Drugs came, experienced a few,
lost for some years, I battle that, too.
I know I called on him when I was too weak to stand,
fell, got up—was all this part of a plan?
For over ten years I ran and ran,
felt my conscience calling out,
Find out what this Jesus is all about.
—Oh heavens, not now, I'm having the fun of my life!
Then one morning filled with strife,
lost control and almost took my life,
That's when Jesus decided the time was right, took my hand,
I'm gonna make this journey right, but first you must surrender,
before you can comprehend my splendor.
How—what do I do? *Forget all the pain inside,*
give it to me, that's why I died.
Ask for forgiveness for all the things and ones you hurt
—complete serenity, that's how it works,
Now open your eyes so I can lead your path,
make your walk straight and erase your past.
Oh if you could only see, what my Jesus has done for me.

Tracey

Daydreaming

Trapped in a world where
White doves do not exist,
I fixed my sight on the wall,
And counted a few of them.
There were four, and one of them
Stood on the edge of my window
And in a soft voice asked me who I was
And what was wrong with me.
Softly I approached her and with the sky
Darkening we started to admire the stars
And I explained about everything in my life.
She says that my worries
Were reflected above me.
Placing her little pink beak
On my cheek, she transformed into
An elegant, beautiful and simple woman.
With a sweet, soft voice she spoke to me
And told me that in reality she was called
Blanca. In surprise I asked her
How could it be true?
She replied that I was
        Daydreaming.

Blanca
translated by Olga Candelario

Yellow

Why do I feel so comfortable with the color yellow? It is like each day you bring out something new in me. Sitting still here I can feel yellow turning on something new in me that I didn't know was there. Could it be because you remind me so much of the sun beating on my skin that keeps me warm all over and lets me feel so alive within?

Oh, Yellow, my toes seem to dance in my shoes. It feels like I am on the lawn, snapping a dandelion between my toes and the flower petals of the dandelion are like one of the most well designed jewels for my toes.

Yellow, why do you bring that tickle feeling on the inside of me to let me know spring is here and summer is close behind? Putting on a yellow dress with my hair down, spinning around on the lawn, the sun keeps beating against my face and gentle breezes keep blowing all over me. Give me one more new adventure today. What part of me will come alive that I did not know existed? Oh, Yellow, keep shining on me.

Princess P.

Who Understands Me But Me
--After Jimmy Santiago Baca

Who understands the language of light that unfolds before
eyes
opened into the dark
when the nose scents the chill morning air?
Stepping down into the well of darkness
outside the front door where
the steps are known by a touch alone
the road is a faint glimmer where at last
I can walk right down the middle
on that line that will be yellow
in the morning, but right now
it is a darkness that fuses
trees and shrubs into looming shadow.
This is my moment along with the earth
when I feel her breath on my cheek and
her flesh resilient under my feet.
There in the secret darkness, I breathe
the many scents of her, the cool green
of grass, the taste of water, and
a rustling in the tree and the sound of something
falling out on outstretched wings, visible
for a heartbeat and then gone.
Who understands that this
is the language of the earth meant
for my senses alone, and how
beneath my feet she lives and breathes.
Who could possibly know as I lean against the four hundred
year maple how necessary I am
for the whole thing to keep going
how necessary we all are.

Ilina

I Am Not

I am not one of what you call Spics.
I am the reminder of your own greed.
The brown-skinned mote in your eye
the ever-present presence in your peripheral vision.
I am not one of the Welfare Cheats.
I am a whole nation of soul and rhythm
which you will never be able to own.
I am one of God's creations.
I am not your janitor or gardener.
I am a woman of power and integrity.
I am a sliver sticking in the side of your conscience.
I am the force that keeps your wheels turning,
your capitalist machinery greased.
I am a voice that tells you
the truths you don't want to hear.
I am the urban legend you can't believe.
I am not what you want me to be.
I am whole and beautiful without your definitions.
The light of my uniqueness rivals the dawn.
I am the wild latina.
I am the salsa-dancer,
I am the sun goddess.
I am the newcomer.
I am the future.

Olga Candelario

I Give You Back

I give you back, Guilt.
You have been my life's companion.
Now you are free to leave.

You kept me company in times of doubt
but I can stand alone now.
Knowing I am free to choose my path
for myself, not for other's or for their needs.
I let go of you willingly, wantonly
and without reservations. I release you
because there is nothing you can do to me
that I have not already done to myself.
Guilt, you had me paralyzed with your doubts
and questionings. I will no longer hold
you close in the midnight wakeful hours.
You are not my secret anymore.
You can't hide inside of me nor can you
torture me with your pokes and jabs.
I no longer feel guilt for being bold,
I no longer feel guilt for being rude.
I no longer feel guilt for being loud
I no longer feel guilt for being me
Yes, you have kept me down,
You have kept me in my place
You kept me in line but now I dance
in circles around you guilt. I am now
my own person and will do
what I decide without looking back,
without second-guessing myself.
Yes, Guilt, I am free and you are still
in your self imposed prison.

Olga Candelario

For The Woman Who
--After Magdalena Gomez

For the woman who
gathers static electricity
& lights the fractured bulbs
fuses watts of energy invisibly
knots twigs into chairs, couches, beds
tables & houses
soaks up pleasure in her lover's bed
then untangles to peel onions & feel the slippery
skin slide away
chops the onion
& throws it in a cast iron pan
where the olive oil glistens

who hammers nails
& hangs art on white walls
donates her willpower to the neighborhood
scratches her lover's name
in wet cement down the block

folds feathery paper
into fireworks
settles chaos like a sleepy child tucked in for the night
hearing frogs, drifts

simmers as she simmers chicken in a pot
breathing steam
whose hair curls in the steam of the simmering chicken
& feels each follicle alive, alive.
This is for the woman who is still alive.

Ellen Miller-Mack

Faluna, My Personal Saint

1.
you were an abandoned baby & i gave you a name.
now you are the queen of my lost & found.
you were wrapped in the hem of a fake fur
at macy's on 34th street.

you were mine to feed & hold in the pediatrics unit at
bellevue, with your mocha skin & tangled hair. at least that's
what you tell me. *faluna*, i whispered. *it's all faluna.*

things return. the turquoise earrings in the snow.
the silver bracelets in between the cushions.
the forgotten something returned to consciousness by you,
faluna.
my mother brought back from the dead
in a set of dice rattling in her red purse tossed down from
your heavens &
tumbling off a high shelf in my closet
with a folded & perfumed white handkerchief, hers.

faluna, you return the dead while I sleep, in a tender collage.
i treasure your sense of humor, your gift for watercolor,
irony, & language.
you are the one who grabs the falling charm as it flies away
from me, who
rummages through bargain bins.

2.
i forget, you remember. i lose, you find.
are you wrapped in all my lost scarves at once, from long
neck to splendid hips?
faluna my hatcheck girl, your hair filled with bobby pins &
rubber bands & ribbons-

the ones i still find in my dreams when you leave them for
me.
faluna my hatcheck girl, my personal saint flashing the
misplaced
returning the lost too soon, the not to be forgotten.
faluna the brown baby in my arms 30 years ago, hostess of
my lost & found.

Ellen Miller-Mack

6:00 AM

Somewhere between pillow and sunlight
cloudy images breeze by,
whisper secrets,
suggest answers to old, old problems.
Colors everywhere blend,
making new shades never seen before.
Nearly familiar voices speak my name.
It is a tender place,
fragile.
I cannot hold it like a snapshot,
or touch it like a falling leaf.
I cannot know it.
It tempts me to stay,
like Dorothy in the Emerald City,
but the tornado of dawn
lands me back in Massachusetts.
With my pen I search
through dream dust
to find a fleck of peace.

Jane Schneeloch

WRITING FROM THE INSIDE

On the first night of the prison writing group, my workshop partner knew her way around the facility like nobody's business, shuttling me through the prison checkpoints, instructing me on the essentials. "Let them stamp your hand, no, your left hand. Wait until he pushes the buzzer. Don't look up at the towers."

When I got home that first night, my house had changed. It was beautiful. The tattered bit of green gingerbread trim beamed at me. So did the rug, and the chair with broken arm. I made a fire. I ate food. I touched everything. Then I sat with Trudy the cat and was grateful to pet her.

Hey, take it easy. I'm the same cat you tossed outside yesterday.

"I went to prison today," I said. Trudy sat as usual, gazing out into the moonlit yard.

"The women there are punished if they look out the windows."

Trudy's tail twitched. She squinted until the pupils of her eyes turned to furious Xs. It's the one thing my cat can relate to, looking out windows. Indoors during the day, she sits in a window, bedazzled by the view.

They can't look out the windows? That's barbaric.

"The guards think they'll make gang signs to other prisoners in other towers." Maybe it was the men who made the gang signs; I couldn't remember. The women seemed to spend most of their time worrying about their children or ill parents or whether their spouses would wait for them. They didn't seem interested in fancy hand signals.

When Trudy sits in the window, she growls at birds and flips her tail back and forth, but she also uses no hand signals. She turned and looked at me.

I would go mad if I couldn't look outside.

"I think they do go mad. But when they write it's a lot like looking out the window."

I have written with the women in prison every week for a year since that first day. Now I know not to look up at the towers. I know that inmates wearing orange haven't been sentenced yet and the ones wearing green are serving designated time. I'm not saying that all these women are wrongly accused. But I also know that the ones wearing orange are in prison because they were too poor to post bail. I know that many of the ones in green, who did break laws, did so because of their bondage to highly addictive drugs. But even without their addictions, these women face many demons. I know this from their writing.

A woman who has had everything imaginable and unimaginable done to her since birth writes unblinkingly about her life. That's her starting place and we all simply stop breathing when she reads. But the place she goes to when she journeys deepest into herself is not the world of razor blades or cat-eyed pimps, but to her deep, inexplicable belief in love.

They write about food, home, family, planting gardens, the men who have beat them, the smell of grandmother's hair. They make funny rhymes, laugh at old boyfriends, long to pee in a bathroom with a door, breathe fresh air. They startle me each week with the honesty and freshness of their voices that have clasped strong fingers around my neck and left me breathless, that have been so sweet all of us have cried. But it is when they write of the blistering damage that has been done to their children that the protective bravado of these women is peeled away. They come undone. I come undone. I'll never forget a haiku written by a young inmate who had lost all rights to both her children because of her drug abuse. The last line, "Hush baby, don't you cry," had too many syllables for a haiku, but by then we weren't counting syllables anymore.

On nights like these, I drive home but hardly remember the trip. I go to bed and toss in my sleep. Their little ones come to me in my dreams and slap at my body with tiny palms. Writing guru Julia Cameron says healing isn't the intention of writing, but only a byproduct. I know what she means, but for the sake of the women writing in prison, I hope the byproduct is bountiful and compassionate.

Jacqueline Sheehan

Guilty Guilty Guilty
Guilty Guilty Guilty

the Corrections Officer proclaims
striding down the hall
towards our writing room.
He is shouting to another guard
stationed behind thick glass.
He is spreading
the news of Kristen Gilbert's verdict.*
He is smiling as he passes.
The words thud
into our soft prison bellies.
One capital Guilty
for each count.
We speak in soft voices,
remembering other murders – one woman's aunt –
other convictions – one woman's son—
this woman who has shared
our space, breathed our re-circulated air.
We contemplate death by execution
and the death of life in prison without parole.
We speak of God's forgiveness,
and we write in sacred silence
after the CO's gloating in the hall.

Six stories down
beneath our window
her bent figure walks
across the prison yard,
lawyer by her side.
His coat blows sideways
as he leads her home.

Kristen Gilbert was convicted of three counts of first degree murder, one count of second degree murder and two counts of attempted murder on March 14, 2003. She had been a nurse at the Veterans' Hospital in Leeds, Massachusetts and because the deaths occurred on federal land she was charged with a capital crime even though the death penalty is not legal in Massachusetts. Later she was sentenced to life without parole.

Carolyn Benson

What I want my words to do to you

I want my words to break your heart and mend it at the same
time,
Pierce the parts of your soul you never knew existed,
Heal old wounds,
Erase present ones.
I want my words to show where I am
Where I have been
And where I'm going.
I want my words to identify that I'm more than what meets
the eye,
Expose my vulnerabilities,
Reveal my strengths.
I want my words to paint a picture,
A Monet or Picasso in written form.
I want my words to change the world,
Make it kinder,
Softer,
Dissolve the hostility,
Break through the bitterness.
I want my words to always be true,
From the heart
And many as the sands of the beach.
I want my words to matter long after my pen lifts off the
page,
My book is shut
And we are no longer together.

Millicent Jackson